I0794133

Our Wonderful World of... Sports

By Rebecca Phillips-Bartlett

KidHaven Publishing

Published in 2024 by
KidHaven Publishing, an Imprint of Greenhaven Publishing, LLC
2544 Clinton St., Buffalo, NY 14224

Written by: Rebecca Phillips-Bartlett
Edited by: Elise Carraway
Designed by: Jasmine Pointer

Photo Credits
Images are courtesy of Shutterstock.com—with thanks to Getty Images, Thinkstock Photo, and iStockphoto.
Recurring images – Naticka, Olga1818. Cover – cosmaa, happy.designer, Mascha Tace, Krafted, GoodStudio, BlueRingMedia, prozaika119, Nadya_Art, Valentina Vectors, VectorsMarket, derter, Rvector, Platinum Photographer, Julinzy, Janathong, Globe Turner, joeni91, Artsem Vysotski, Olga1818, funkyplayer. 2–3 – Volodymyr Burdiak. 4–5 – Djent, noir_illustration. 6–7 – Fotokvadrat, James A Boardman, Droidworker, curiosity, Anatolir. 8–9 –Chrispictures, Andrey Burmakin, ProStockStudio, mejorana. 10–11 – Frederic Legrand - COMEO, FamVeld, Alisa ChaseOn, jennylipets, baldezh, Kristina Chistiakova. 12–13 – Ivan Smuk, Wadyab Pico, tcharts, Viktorija Reuta, T-Kot. 14–15 – oliveromg, LightField Studios, IfH, Kate Zimneva, Hut Hanna. 16–17 – CHEN WS, iconriver, Belish, klyaksun. 18–19 – Mizkit, Shahjehan, Nach-Noth, Artsholic, The img. 20–21 – Paolo Bona, simez78, matrioshka, Incomible, joeni91.

Cataloging-in-Publication Data
Names: Phillips-Bartlett, Rebecca, 1999-.
Title: Sports / Rebecca Phillips-Bartlett.
Description: Buffalo, New York: KidHaven Publishing, 2024. |
Series: Our wonderful world of… | Includes glossary and index.
Identifiers: ISBN 9781534546233 (pbk.) | ISBN 9781534546240 (library bound) | ISBN 9781534546257 (ebook)
Subjects: LCSH: Sports--Juvenile literature.
Classification: LCC GV705.4 P487 2024 | DDC 796--dc23

Manufactured in the United States of America

CPSIA compliance information: Batch #CW24KH: For further information contact Greenhaven Publishing LLC at 1-844-317-7404.

CONTENTS

Words that look like <u>this</u> can be found in the glossary on page 24.

WELCOME TO OUR WONDERFUL WORLD!

Our world is wonderful. Around the world, many people love sports. Some countries have a national sport. This is a sport that is an important part of a country's culture.

Let's go on a tour around the world! In each country, we will meet a guide. They will tell us about the sports people play in their country.

DID YOU KNOW?

Soccer is the most played and watched sport in the world.

CANADA

Ice Hockey

Ice hockey is often thought of as one of the fastest games on Earth. The teams try to get a puck into the other team's goal. They do this all while skating on ice.

Lacrosse

Lacrosse is known as the oldest team sport in North America. It is one of Canada's national sports. Lacrosse players move a ball across a field and try to score a goal.

DID YOU KNOW?

A lacrosse stick is also called a crosse.

CUBA

Baseball

Baseball is Cuba's national sport. It is a team game. The teams take turns being batters and fielders. Batters hit the ball as far as they can. Fielders try to catch it.

Dance

Dance is sometimes like a sport! Cuba is known for many different styles of dance, such as salsa and rumba. Salsa and rumba are often performed with two dancers who are partners.

THE UNITED KINGDOM

Rowing

Hi, I am Olivia. I live in the United Kingdom.

Rowing is a water sport. Rowers use long paddles, called oars, to move their boat through the water. People can row alone or as part of a team, called a crew.

Motorsports

Motorsports involve racing vehicles, such as cars and motorcycles. These are some of the fastest vehicles in the world. Big races include the popular Formula 1 car races.

DID YOU KNOW?

Formula 1 races can last up to 2 hours!

FRANCE

Cycling

Every year, France holds a huge bicycle race called the Tour de France. This race lasts three weeks. Each day, the person who is in the lead wears a special yellow jersey.

Skiing

Skiing is a winter sport in France. Skiers use long, thin boards, called skis, to slide over the snow. They hold poles to help them balance and to push themselves along as they race down mountains.

SOUTH AFRICA

Hello! My name is Lethabo. I live in South Africa.

Cricket

Cricket is played with two teams. The batter stands in front of a set of sticks called a wicket. The bowler on the other team tries to knock the wicket down with a ball, which the batter tries to hit away.

Soccer

Soccer is a very popular sport in South Africa. Most players kick the ball with their feet. The goalkeepers are the only people who are allowed to touch the ball with their hands.

CHINA

Table Tennis

Table tennis is one of China's national sports. It is played on a table with a net across the middle. Players use a paddle to hit the ball back and forth across the table.

Gymnastics

There are many different types of gymnastics. Gymnasts need to have very good balance and flexibility. Gymnastics is sometimes performed on a special floor. This floor helps gymnasts bounce higher and avoid getting hurt.

DID YOU KNOW?

Some gymnasts use props such as ribbons or balls.

MALAYSIA

Hi! I am Amaal. I live in Malaysia.

Badminton

To play badminton, players use a racket to hit a shuttlecock over a net. A shuttlecock is cone shaped. This shape helps it move through the air very quickly, so players have to be fast!

shuttlecock

Sepak Takraw

Sepak takraw is Malaysia's national sport. Players have to jump very high to kick a ball over a net. They cannot touch the ball with their hands or arms.

NEW ZEALAND

Rugby

Rugby is a contact sport. This means that the players can push, shove, or tackle each other to get the ball. When passing the ball, players can't throw the ball forward.

Hi, my name is Lucas.
I live in New Zealand.

Netball

Netball is played by two teams of seven. Each player has a different job and can only go to certain parts of the court. To score, a player throws the ball into a net.

A WORLD OF SUPER SPORTS

On our tour, we have discovered lots of super sports. Some of these sports are popular in many different countries, while others are only played in some places.

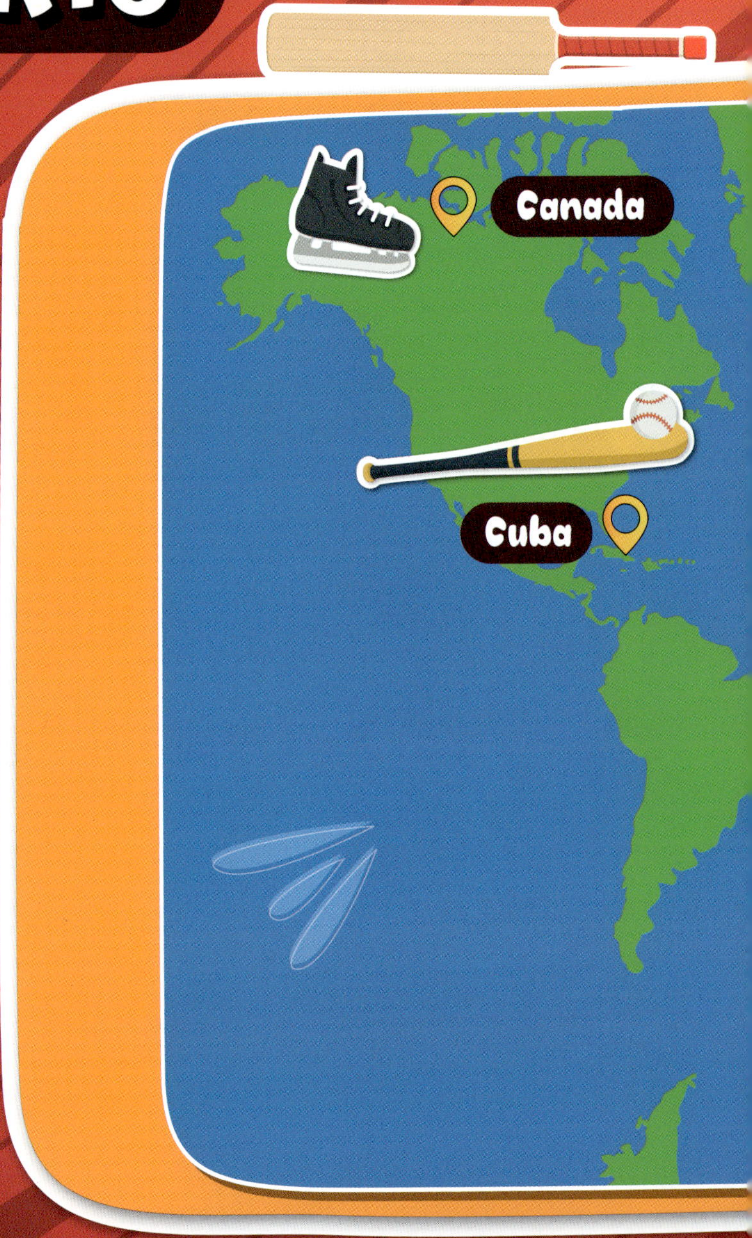

Wherever you live, super sports are played there too. Imagine you are a tour guide. If someone came to your country for a tour, what sport would you tell them about?

GLOSSARY

balance	to stay upright
court	an area with four sides used for playing a sport with a ball
culture	the traditions, ideas, and ways of life of a group of people
flexibility	the ability to bend and stretch the body
performed	shown in front of an audience
props	objects used as part of a show or performance
puck	a small rubber disc used in ice hockey
racket	a tool with a handle and a net stretched over a round or oval frame that is used to hit an object in a sport
tackle	to stop another player by knocking them to the ground
tour	a trip that involves visiting many different places

INDEX